Christmas 2002 –

To My Dearest Colette –

California Here We Come.

With Lots of Love –

Mum –

# The
# Fragrant Year

David & Charles

# The Fragrant Year

Seasonal Inspirations
for a Scent-filled Home

**CLARE LOUISE HUNT**

*photography by*
**Shona Wood**

David & Charles

A DAVID & CHARLES BOOK

First published in the UK in 2000 by David & Charles

A catalogue record for this book is available from the
British Library.

ISBN 0 7153 1076 3

This book was conceived and produced by
Breslich & Foss Ltd
20 Wells Mews
London W1P 3FJ

For David & Charles
Brunel House
Newton Abbot
Devon

Printed in Singapore

C O N T E N T S

Our sense of smell is probably the sense that we most take for granted. Although we are aware of everyday odors, from toast in the morning to traffic fumes on the way to work, it is easy to overlook the less obvious impact a healthy sense of smell has on our lives. Smells are evocative stimuli and can be powerfully reminiscent of places and events. Who does not have a particular smell that, when registered, can take him or her straight back to schooldays, or to a pivotal point in their life? A sense of smell connects a newborn baby to its mother, attracts potential partners to each other, and can even influence our choice of a new home.

An assault on any of our senses can make us uncomfortable; by contrast, we can be soothed, comforted and restored to equanimity by exposure to positive stimuli: music is calming and uplifting, a beautiful sight can take our breath away, a massage can relax us. Similarly, delicious scents can awaken in us feelings of comfort, tranquility, and even euphoria.

This book is packed with ideas for bringing fragrance into your home. You will find plenty of simple projects that will fill your home with refreshing, relaxing, comforting, or stimulating aromas to suit your changing mood throughout the year. Whatever the season, you can fill your house with the scent of homemade potpourri; make bathtime a treat by adding herbs and essential oils to the water; lie back and relax among scented pillows and cushions, and entertain your guests with delicious and aromatic food and drink. Fragrant herbs, flowers, and oils have been treasured for centuries for their healing and soothing qualities; I hope that the following pages will inspire you to bring all kinds of delicious scents into your home.

# spring

*rintemps · vår · primavera*

At the end of winter, as our senses are at their most jaded, a whisper of warm wind, a glimpse of blue in the sky, and a faint hint of spring flowers can bring our joie de vivre flooding back. Spring is a time of boundless energy, exuberance, optimism, and new life. The scent of spring flowers abounds, and a general freshness pervades the air as winter fades, bringing with it a desire to exchange rich, heavy colors and fragrances for soft pastel hues and fresh, crisp scents.

*imavera · forår · voorjaar*

L I V I N G   R O O M

Use fresh flowers to decorate your dining table. A delightful display can be made by placing a candle within a circle of florist's foam, and adding sweet-smelling flowers such as jonquils and freesias. The simplicity of these flowers adds to their charm, so an informal arrangement works best. Keep the foam moist, and the display will last several days.

# LIVING ROOM

Create an invigorating potpourri with the dried petals or whole blossoms of colorful flowers such as jonquils, daffodils, pansies, and violets. Add strips of lemon and lime peel, and scent the mixture with uplifting oils such as grapefruit, juniper, lemon verbena and rosemary. You will find instructions for making potpourri on pages 128-9.

K I T C H E N

With the advent of warmer weather, even the most reluctant gardener feels the pull of the outdoors, although you don't need a garden to enjoy the luxury of fresh herbs. Herbs are an essential part of good cooking, adding their unique flavors to many a recipe. Add fresh herbs to bottles of oil and vinegar, leave them for a few months, and you'll find that the oils and vinegars have absorbed the aromas and flavors of the plants.

**Spring is the time to plant fragrant herbs such as basil and rosemary. Pots of herbs on a sunny windowsill bring the freshness and color of the garden into the home.**

# KITCHEN

Fresh herbs have been highly valued for their medicinal properties for centuries. An easy way to enjoy the benefits of peppermint – which is said to aid digestion – is to make it into a tea. Simply steep fresh, clean leaves in boiling water and add sugar or honey to taste for a refreshing and delicious alternative to tea or coffee.

Keep your pantry well stocked with dried herbs – even the best herb garden may not yield the right herb for every recipe. Adding a vanilla pod to a storage jar of sugar will give you vanilla-scented sugar; candied angelica root has many decorative uses; try to stock whole cinnamon sticks and nutmegs along with the ground variety of each.

At teatime, or for snacks, experiment with old-fashioned recipes that rely on natural ingredients for their flavor, such as caraway-seed cake, honey biscuits, gingersnaps, and poppy-seed loaves. This lemon cake is deliciously moist and has a mouth-wateringly tangy flavor. For a special treat, dip mint leaves and lemon slices in egg white and granulated sugar, allow to dry, then use to garnish the top of the cake. See page 137 for the recipe.

23

**A walk though a shady woodland bursting with delicately scented flowers is one of the joys of the new season.**

# KITCHEN

One of the first signs that spring has truly arrived is the sight of flowers pushing their way skyward. Bring the freshness of spring indoors by planting window boxes with springtime blooms, such as daffodils and bluebells, and filling tubs and other containers with scented flowers such as this *Primula auricula*, a scented variety of primrose.

Slip dried lavender
bunches, bound and cased
in delicate muslin, between
stacks of folded linen.

Store your favorite
nightgown in a charming
gingham case scented
with potpourri.

Along with that new lease on life that tends to accompany this welcome season comes the urge to spring clean. If you yearn for order, clearing out closets and eliminating unwanted clothes and junk is a positively liberating experience. Freshen your linen closet with the simple projects shown here. How-to instructions can be found on page 136-7.

**Freshen your closet by hanging pretty citrus pouches on coat hangers.**

LINEN CLOSET

Winter perfumes are often too heavy for the sunnier seasons, so switch to a lighter, fresher fragrance containing floral and citrus notes as the weather changes. Rather than soaking in hot, oil-scented bathtubs, try a shower for an invigorating alternative. A body splash made with citrus oil will give you that "zest for life" in the mornings. Grapefruit oil has light, fruity fresh notes, and is said to stimulate feelings of euphoria, lightness and well-being – perfect if you feel a little tired when you get up. How-to instructions are on page 138.

BATHROOM

Combine dried herbs and flowers in a muslin bath bag and hang it over the hot-water faucet. The running water will carry the delicate scents of the plants into the bathtub. Add cold water to bring the bath to a comfortable temperature, and leave the bag in the water while you are enjoying your scented bath. See "Bathtime" on pages 133-4 for how-to instructions.

Burning candles that have been scented with essential oils is a treat whatever the time of day or year. These pale blue candles are scented with juniper oil, which has a fresh, fruity fragrance, and whose effects are uplifting, stimulating and refreshing. Oils can be used alone or you can mix two or three together to make a blend to suit your mood. You will find instructions for making all kinds of candles on pages 126-7.

To make a stunning Valentine's Day bouquet to present to your sweetheart, choose flowers that have a sweet fragrance and delicate beauty. Grape hyacinths and daffodils make a delightfully fragrant combination. Gather the flowers into a pleasing arrangement and tie the stems tightly together with floral tape. Wrap a sheet of cellophane around the flowers and slip a rubber band over the stems. Trim the cellophane to the desired size, and decorate the bouquet with a ribbon.

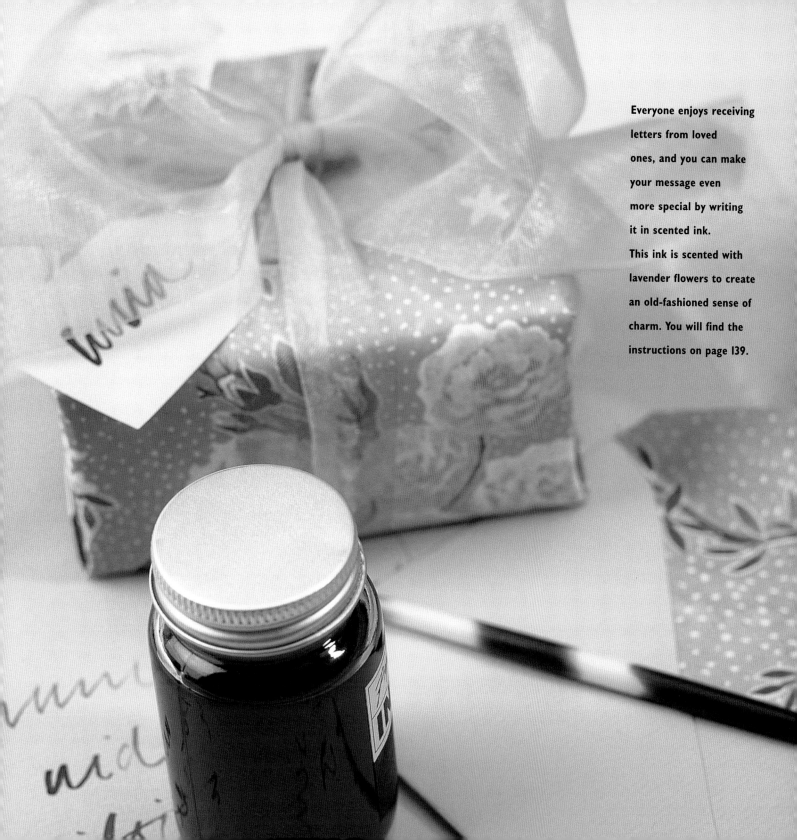

Everyone enjoys receiving
letters from loved
ones, and you can make
your message even
more special by writing
it in scented ink.
This ink is scented with
lavender flowers to create
an old-fashioned sense of
charm. You will find the
instructions on page 139.

verano · estate · zomer · é

*summer*

estate · summer · été · vera

Summertime stretches lazily across the year, conjuring up thoughts of huge blue skies, ripe fruits, and fresh flowers. The scents of summer are dewy roses in the early morning, newly mown hay, salty breezes from the sea mingled with the smell of suntan lotions, heat rising from shimmering streets, plump strawberries, and ice cream cones clutched in children's hot little hands.

Now is the time to harvest aromatic flowers and herbs that will form part of the potpourris that in turn will create a wonderful atmosphere in your home when the weather turns autumnal.

Make place settings special by tying a fresh rose
to each napkin with a pretty bow.
Add charm to a wedding table with a stunning
floral swag. Instructions on how to make this
gorgeous garland are on page 140.

*summer*

# LIVING ROOM

**Summer is the time to harvest rose petals that will be the base of your potpourris.**

To create this stunning display, arrange pebbles in a glass bowl filled with fresh water. The rose stems will be held in place by the stones. Insert the central roses first, then continue to add flowers until the bowl is full.

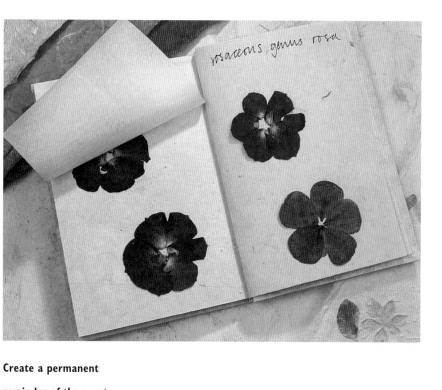

rosaceous genus rosa

**Create a permanent reminder of the scents and colors of summer by pressing your favorite flowers. Full instructions are on page 143.**

Plant large tubs and window boxes with white jasmine (*Jasminum officinale*), whose tiny flowers give off an enchanting fragrance. Throw open windows to allow the delicious scent to waft into your home. If you have a garden, plant scented herbs such as thyme and lawn camomile in cracks in paths and terraces as a clever way to perfume the air: the leaves yield wonderful scents when crushed underfoot.

Although sweet peas last only a few days once cut, their delicate scent and exquisite shapes make them an ideal flower for a simple bouquet. Trim the stems to the required length and bind them tightly together with floral tape. Wrap the arrangement in two contrasting sheets of tissue paper, holding them in place around the base with raffia or a length of ribbon tied in a bow.

SPECIAL

OCCASIONS

**Serve your guests
fragrant dishes redolent
of summer, such as flower
and mixed herb salads,
herb-y breads, luscious
tomatoes fresh from
the vine, bowls of ripe
summer fruits, and
delicately scented sorbets
and ice creams.**

KITCHEN

Ice bowls look stunning when filled with summer
fruits such as these plump strawberries. As an
alternative to freezing whole rosebuds in the ice,
single petals can be used. There are full
instructions for making ice bowls on page 140.

Make a simple dish of ice cream special by topping each serving with sugar-frosted rose petals (you'll find instructions on page 140). For an added touch of luxury, scatter fresh rose petals on the dining table.

Homemade lemonade
spiked with fresh mint
leaves is the perfect
cooling drink on a hot
summer's day.

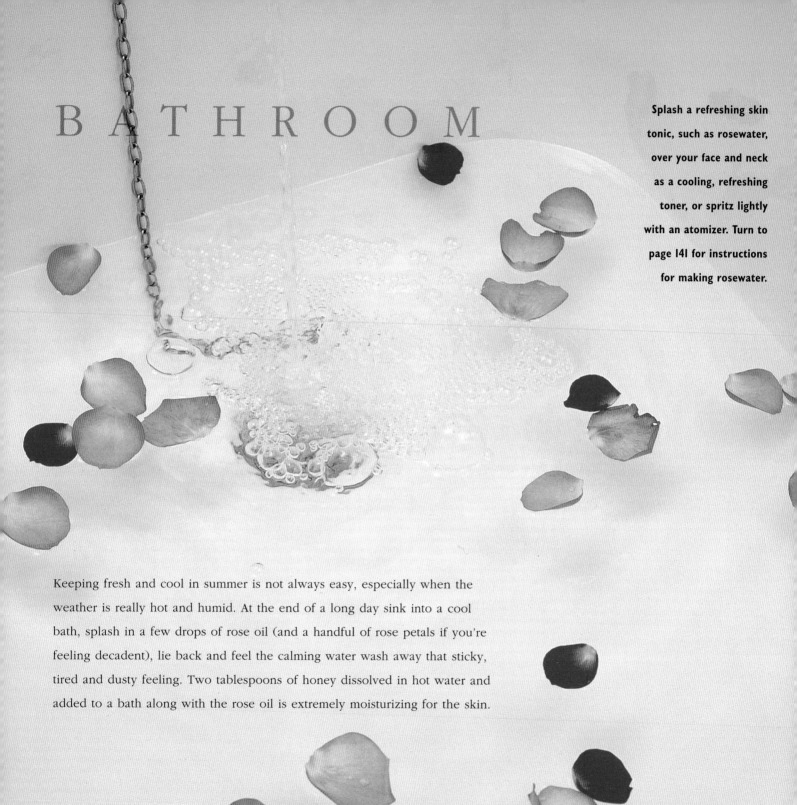

# BATHROOM

Splash a refreshing skin tonic, such as rosewater, over your face and neck as a cooling, refreshing toner, or spritz lightly with an atomizer. Turn to page 141 for instructions for making rosewater.

Keeping fresh and cool in summer is not always easy, especially when the weather is really hot and humid. At the end of a long day sink into a cool bath, splash in a few drops of rose oil (and a handful of rose petals if you're feeling decadent), lie back and feel the calming water wash away that sticky, tired and dusty feeling. Two tablespoons of honey dissolved in hot water and added to a bath along with the rose oil is extremely moisturizing for the skin.

These organdy panels are easy to sew, and they make delightful room dividers. Alternatively, hang them in front of a muslin curtain to add interest to a room. Slip scented dried petals between the panels and enjoy the delicate fragrance as you pass by – because they are made of such light, airy fabric they stir in the slightest breeze. Instructions for making the panels are given on page 141

LINEN
CLOSET

**Plant honeysuckle, old roses, night-scented stock, and nicotiana, to scent the air at dusk.**

Scattering your home with potpourri-filled cushions will ensure that you can enjoy the scent of roses even if you don't have a garden. Choose a pretty floral fabric for the cushion cover; fill it with a slightly smaller cushion and a sachet of your favorite blend of summer potpourri. Use only the softest petals so that there are no hard lumps to make the cushion uncomfortable. See "Cushions and Sachets" and page 142 for how-to instructions.

A wreath of fresh roses makes an exquisite decoration. Cut the rose stems and press the flower heads into a foam base that has been soaked in water. Add sprigs of honeysuckle for extra fragrance.

Hang heart-shaped rose pomanders above your bed or in the linen closet. If you scent the rosebuds with essential oils (see page 129), their fragrance will linger for the whole summer. Turn to page 143 for instructions on making the pomanders.

(see page 129), ... Turn to page 143

LINEN CLOSET

A bunch of lavender, hyssop, southernwood, and dried garden roses will bring a subtle fragrance to the linen closet, and help ward off moths. Bind the stems with wire, then conceal the wire with a bow.

höst · *najar* · autumn · *otoñ*

*autumn*

herbst · autumn · efterår · *a*

Long, hazy days gradually become shorter and the air takes on a new vigor as summer blends into autumn. The scents of freshly mown grass and flowers in full bloom give way to those of just-picked apples, rain-soaked fields and bonfires of burning leaves. Every season has its own exclusive cocktail of evocative scents, and autumn is no exception: the rich earthy smell of damp leaves kicked underfoot, the faint whiff of woodsmoke on the wind, and the sweet snap and crackle of caramelized sugar on a candied apple.

No sofa or armchair is complete without the luxury of a few cushions to sink into after a long day. You can design and make your own cushions, or slip a potpourri sachet between the cover and the inner pillow of a ready-made one. You'll find a recipe for an aromatic blend of flowers and oils on page 144.

# KITCHEN

Aside from smelling and tasting delicious, apples can be used to make attractive decorations that will lend a charming, rustic feel to your kitchen. The dried slices have a delicate apple scent all their own, but you can add a spicy aroma to them. Lightly wrap the dried slices in cotton cloths that have been dotted with drops of cinnamon oil, and leave them for a few weeks before stringing them together. Instructions are on page 144.

Twig balls like these can be scented by placing them in a plastic bag and scattering them with a few drops of fragrant oil. After two or three weeks, the balls will have absorbed the scent. Try bergamot or sandalwood for warm, autumnal aromas. Decorate the balls with ribbons, and display in a simple wooden bowl.

# LIVING ROOM

Take advantage of the harvest season and chase away the autumnal chill by filling your kitchen with the delicious, heart-warming smells that come from home baking. Nothing can quite surpass the feeling of well-being created by delicious aromas that promise mouthwatering delights. Homemade apple pie is always a favorite; served piping hot and topped with crème Anglaise or heavy cream, it's an unbeatable treat for family and friends.

# KITCHEN

When autumn fruits are in abundance, set aside a few hours to capture their fruity goodness in homemade preserves. Jam-making will fill your kitchen with sharp, tangy flavors and make breakfast or snack time a real treat. Why not bake some bread, too, and let the delicious smell permeate every corner of the house?

K I T C H E N

The scent and taste of candied apples are reminiscent of Halloween and bonfire parties. The smell of caramel bubbling on the stove evokes memories of exciting nighttime festivities. Rosy red flavorful apples coated with candy are guaranteed to set children's eyes aglow. For a more sophisticated look, wrap the candied apples in bright red cellophane. You'll find instructions for all the autumn recipes on pages 145-7.

When there's a slight nip in the air it's nice to welcome guests with piping-hot spiced cider. What's more, a large pan of fragrant mulling ingredients will create a warm, inviting atmosphere in the kitchen.

KITCHEN

Drawer liners lightly scented with your favorite herbs are very easy to make, and will prevent clothes from smelling musty over the coming winter months. Cut sheets of paper to the size of the drawer and place them in a plastic bag with a potpourri sachet (see page 130). Leave for two to three weeks. Try to choose handmade paper that contains flower petals or leaves; it is especially pretty.

Sew dried rose petals or a fine potpourri mixture into little muslin pouches to make charming pillow sachets. These are perfect for guest bedrooms – they ensure that spare beds remain as fresh and sweet to sleep in as they were the day they were made. The cocktail of oils and potpourri given in the recipe on page 147 was chosen for its sleep-inducing qualities.

When you pull out warm clothes that have been stored over the summer, there is nothing worse than discovering that the moths got there first. Camphor mothballs may be unattractive to moths, but they are equally unattractive to us. Lavender is a good, natural moth deterrent and, what's more, it infuses clothes with a delicious fragrance. Sew up a few small velvet sachets, fill them with dried lavender, and decorate with little glass beads. Your drawers will not only smell wonderful, but will look wonderful too. Turn to page 148 for a potpourri recipe.

When it's too cold outside to have the windows open, keep the atmosphere fresh by placing bowls of potpourri around your home. Add an autumnal twist to the ingredients by using dried corn cobs and pinecones collected from the woods to give the potpourri a chunkier feel; add pretty Chinese lanterns for extra color. Choose oils that create a feeling of warmth and security, such as those suggested in the recipe on page 148.

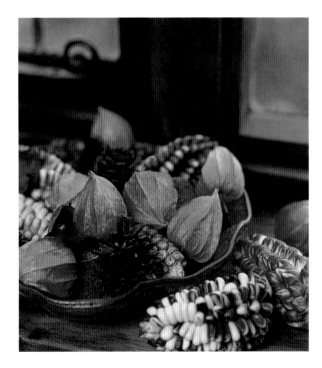

BEDROOM

Coats and jackets stored over the winter months will keep their shape far better when hung on good coat hangers. Padded coat hangers are kinder to fabrics and fine tailoring, and if you scent the padding, both closet and clothes will smell of your favorite essential oils. Instructions for making a padded coat hanger can be found on page 148.

Shoes can develop a peculiar smell all their own, despite the best efforts of their owners, so add a little luxury to your shoes by filling them with scented slipper sachets (see page 149). Shoes retain their shape much better if they're stuffed with something, so these pretty shoe sachets are doubly practical.

HALLWAY

# BATHROOM

Nothing is as luxurious as a bath, so spoil yourself with bathroom treats throughout the year. For autumn, make some delightful handmade soaps for the sink. For that seasonal touch, use warm colors for the ingredients, and choose rich, comforting fragrances such as orange, orange blossom and cinnamon. Orange oils are valued for their warm, sensuous attributes, and are wonderful for creating a positive ambiance. For how-to instructions, turn to page 149.

Although summer is over, there are still plenty of
flowers to be found should you yearn for a fresh
floral arrangement. Late roses mixed with autumn
berries make stunning displays for the dinner table.
Choose warm autumnal colors that complement the
time of year and add a cheerful glow to the room.

**Delight a friend with a letter written on scented paper (see page 78). To make an envelope, unfold an existing one and trace around it onto a piece of paper to give you the pattern from which to fold your own envelope. Cut the notepaper into sheets, and slip a few dried rose petals in with your message.**

The beautiful, fragrant blooms of summer soon fade, but you can enjoy them all year round by drying and pressing flower heads and petals. To make these simple arrangements, hang selected roses upside down in a dry place and leave them until all the moisture has evaporated from the petals. Cut the stems to a few inches long, then place the flowers in a plastic bag with a few drops of rose essential oil. Leave for a couple of weeks, then press the stems into a florist's dry foam ball placed in a flowerpot. If the scent begins to fade it can be refreshed by sprinkling some more fragrant oil onto the rose heads.

There is nothing quite like a steaming cup of hot chocolate to bring the color back to one's cheeks after a brisk walk in the woods. Melt chunks of rich, dark chocolate in a saucepan with a little hot water. Gradually add milk, stirring all the time. If the chocolate is quite bitter, you might need to add sugar. For extra luxury, add a dollop of whipped cream just before serving.

# KITCHEN

**Freshly ground coffee has a seductive aroma all its own. For best results, grind the beans just before making the coffee.**

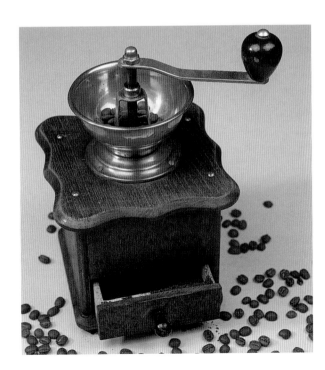

vinter · *invierno* · winte

*winter*

winter · *hiver* · vinter · *i*

# *hiver · vinter · inverno*

As winter draws near and Christmas approaches, we long for warm, comfortable interiors. Our senses yearn for the heat and light missing since the end of summer, and we are seduced by rich dark colors, warm indulgent foods, soft sensuous fabrics, and the spicy, heady scents that remind us of the good things in the winter months. The exotic smell of mulling wine infused with cloves, cinnamon sticks, and ginger, the distinctive seasonal fragrances of Christmas trees and pinecones – all these scents combine to create a feeling of security and well-being. Experienced unexpectedly and in isolation they can take us straight back to our fondest winter memories.

*...verno · vinter · invierno*

S P E C I A L

The Christmas tree has a particularly evocative scent all of its own, but you can add to this by making your own decorations. Whole lemons and limes will bring a zesty added bonus to the tree. Cinnamon bundles add that holiday smell and, finally, spicy ginger cookies make the tree almost impossible to admire without pausing to indulge the sense of smell.

O C C A S I O N S

Gift-wrap your presents simply, but make them completely original by decorating them with ribbons and dried herbs and flowers. Use small bouquets of lavender, roses, and other dried scented flowers, or tie up small bunches of fragrant herbs, such as rosemary and bay leaves, and tuck the stems into the top of the bow.

S P E C I A L

O C C A S I O N S

L I V I N G  R O O M

These delightful
decorations are easy to
make and smell divine.
Score firm limes with
a sharp knife, then place
them in a low oven (about
250°F) until completely
dried. Once cool, store
them for a couple of
days in a plastic bag into
which you have scattered
a few drops of tangy
citrus oil.

Fresh citrus scents lift the spirits and stimulate the senses at a time when the cold weather and dark nights can cause spirits to droop. A table display of carved limes is a treat to behold, offering both an uplifting color and an energizing, tangy fragrance. Use the grooved blade of a linoleum-cutting tool (available from crafts stores) to create simple designs in firm fruit. Painting the scored lines with lemon or lime juice will prevent them from becoming brown. Clove-studded limes add to the display, and the cloves bring a warm, sweet and spicy aroma to the fruits. Use a skewer to make the holes in the limes before inserting the whole cloves.

LIVING

ROOM

Bundles of cinnamon sticks make attractive and unusual Christmas decorations. Cut all the cinnamon sticks to the same length with a pair of kitchen scissors. Fasten four or five sticks together with tightly wound fine wire, leaving a loop at the end. Conceal the wire with a length of ribbon, then hang the bundles on your tree.

These star-shaped ginger cookies make a deliciously different addition to the Christmas tree. Make sure that you bake plenty – they are irresistible to passers-by! You'll find the recipe on page 150.

LIVING ROOM

Candles are very atmospheric; they soften and calm the environment while bringing a sense of intimacy to your home. Burning scented candles releases essential oils into the air, instantly transforming the mood of any room. Depending on the fragrance you choose, you can create a sensual, stimulating, or relaxing mood. See "Scented Candles" on pages 126-7 for how-to instructions.

During wintertime, we can afford to indulge ourselves in the heavier, richer scents that we associate with warmth, coziness and good cheer. Frankincense, amber, geranium, clove and orange all conjure up the magic of Christmas.

Enhance the effect of scented candles by glueing fragrant petals to the candle holders (see page 129 for how to scent petals). As the candle burns, the aroma of the wax and the scented blossoms will mingle and scent the air.

Give every room in the house a distinctive fragrance by creating your own special blend of winter potpourri: try a combination of evocative scents such as cinnamon, lavender, orange and lime. Turn to page 151 for a recipe.

LIVING ROOM

# LIVING ROOM

Pinecones collected from outdoor walks, then sprayed white and silver and piled high in a charming bowl make a beautiful and festive arrangement. Prepare the cones by storing them for a week in a plastic bag into which drops of the spicy, sweet-smelling oils of cinnamon and clove have been added. Spray them lightly with fake snow, and sprinkle them with glitter while still damp before piling them up into a simple but richly scented display.

Not all the fragrances in your home during the winter months need be from essential oils: hyacinths make beautiful winter blooms – and their heady, intoxicating scent can pervade even the largest areas.

LIVING ROOM

Burning incense sticks
is an inexpensive way to
scent a room.

One of the most comforting rituals at any time of the year is taking a bath – and when the weather is particularly punishing and you feel cold through to the bone, only a hot bath will really warm you up. Allow yourself time to indulge in the tub, and mix a few drops of essential oil with a fragrance-free liquid soap to create a luxurious soak.

Most of us will suffer from uncomfortable blocked noses and colds at some point during winter; making use of certain fragrances will ease the problem. Adding a few drops of oils such as angelica, eucalyptus, cypress, mountain pine, and juniper to the bath water is said to soothe colds and make breathing easier. See "Bathtime" on pages 133-4 for how-to instructions.

# LINEN CLOSET

Make a classic orange and clove pomander to continue the spicy theme right into the linen closet. Choose a firm, thick-skinned orange and use a skewer to punch holes in the fruit before inserting the cloves. Tie a ribbon firmly around the orange, leaving a loop so you can hang it up.

The bedroom should be a peaceful and sensual haven. Fill it with items that delight the senses: sumptuous textures, calming colors, relaxing shapes and sensuous, sleep-inducing fragrances. A good night's sleep is essential to our well-being; the frenetic pace of a busy day should always be soothed away before you go to sleep. Scented pillows (see page 151) made from rich, soft velvets in gorgeous colors are the perfect nighttime companions. Fill a potpourri sachet with your favorite herbal mixture for a good night's sleep and sweet dreams. For a sleep-inducing effect use geranium, honey oil, lavender, and mimosa. Orange and nutmeg are said to bring happy dreams; jasmine, ylang-ylang and patchouli are famed for their aphrodisiac qualities!

Winter is a time to indulge
and take comfort in rich,
warming foods that keep
spirits high and help us ward
off chilly weather. A rich,
fruity steamed pudding is
a special treat.

There is nothing quite like the spicy aroma of piping-hot mulled
wine to chase away the chill of crisp winter evenings. Our classic
recipe (page 153) includes the pungent flavors of cinnamon,
cloves, and fresh oranges.

To make a spectacular holiday wreath, begin with a pine-covered base and add scented decorations. You can usually purchase ready-made pine wreaths from florists at Christmastime, but you can also make one yourself: instructions are given in "Wreaths" on page 132.

Decorate with whatever fresh aromatic herbs are available – rosemary is perfect. Tuck in cinnamon sticks, dried citrus slices, pomegranates, apples or aromatic mandarin oranges, and cloves; arrange them within the foliage. Fresh fruit will keep for up to a couple of weeks, but if you want your wreath to last well into the New Year, use dried fruit, or specially made pomanders.

HALLWAY

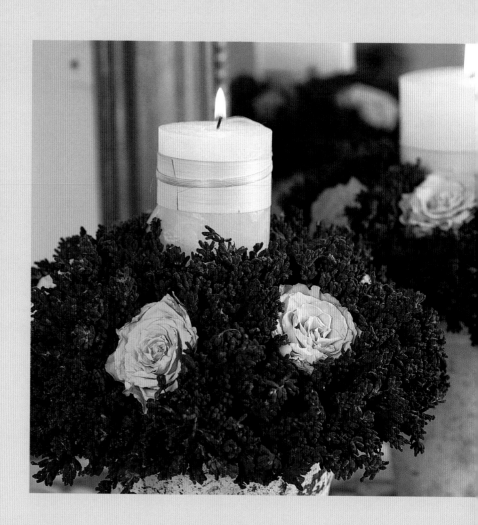

HALLWAY

Make your home warm and inviting by
burning scented candles in the hallway.
Beeswax candles release a delicious,
honey-tinged fragrance as they burn. To
create the arrangement shown here, place
a beeswax candle within a ring of florist's
foam in a pot. Insert dried, scented
roses (see page 129) at regular intervals
around the candle. Add sprigs of fragrant
lavender so that the foam is completely
hidden. To enhance the effect, place your
arrangement in front of a mirror. The
aroma of scented candles, combined with
enticing smells from the kitchen, sets the
scene for any festive occasion.

## SCENTED CANDLES

Nowadays, it is easy to buy all kinds of scented candles, but it is fun to make your own as well. Bear in mind that the wax becomes very hot and should never be touched until cool; always check the temperature with a suitable thermometer – don't just guess it. Always heat the wax in a container over water, not directly on the heat. If the wax begins to smoke, turn off the heat and let cool.

## Container candles

*paraffin wax*  
*stearin*  
*glass container*  
*measuring jug*  
*wick*  
*wick sustainer*  

*wax dye*  
*candle scent*  
*double boiler*  
*wax thermometer*  
*skewer or toothpick*  

**1** Paraffin wax is odorless, and glossy and transparent when set. However, it will burn very fast if used alone. To counter this, small amounts of another kind of wax, called stearin, need to be added. As a general rule, you will need 90 percent paraffin wax and 10 percent stearin.

**2** To find out how much wax and stearin you will need, pour water into your container to the required height of the candle, then pour the water into a measuring jug. For every ½ cup (100ml) water, you will need about 3oz (90g) cold wax.

**3** Choose a slightly smaller wick than you would use for a free-standing candle. To prime the wick, tie a loop at one end and dip the wick in molten wax. Hold it there for a few seconds, then remove, pull straight and hang to dry. Place one end of the wick in a wick sustainer.

# *Instructions*

**4** Melt the stearin in the top half of a double boiler and fill the bottom half with hot water. Alternatively, you can use a saucepan placed inside a larger one. Place on a medium heat. When the stearin has completely melted and turned into a clear liquid, gradually add tiny amounts of dye.

**5** Add the wax to this mixture and place the double boiler over a medium heat. Add the candle scent and heat to 180°F (82°C).

**6** Fix the wick sustainer to the bottom of the container with a little of the molten wax. Wrap the other end of the wick around a skewer so that it is held taut in the center of the container. Carefully pour the scented wax into the container to within ½ in (1cm) of the desired height of your candle. (You should have a little wax left over.) Tap the sides of the glass to release trapped air bubbles and leave until almost set.

**7** As the wax cools it will contract. Wait until a thick skin has formed on the surface, then make holes in it and pour in the remainder of the wax, reheated to the correct temperature. You may have to do this more than once before the surface of the candle is completely flat. Let cool, then trim the wick to the required size.

## POTPOURRI

The translation of "potpourri" is rotten pot, a reference to the original method of making it, in which flowers are semi-dried and fermented in a large crock. This is known as the moist method, and it results in a strongly scented potpourri. The more modern method is the dry method. Potpourri made this way is very attractive, because the individual ingredients retain their shape, but is not as fragrant.

## Moist method

*3 cups rose petals*
*½ cup coarse sea salt*
*dried grated rind of ½ an orange or lemon*
   *(optional)*
*3 tbsp dried herbs of your choosing*
*2 tbsp ground spices of your choosing*

**I** Roses always form the base of a moist potpourri. Gather them on a dry day when the flowers have just fully opened. Pull off the petals and spread them out to dry on any flat surface that is perforated to allow air to circulate. A metal rack or a shallow basket would be ideal. Keep different colors apart to avoid staining. Either dry the petals outdoors in the hot sun or indoors in a warm, airy room. For a moist potpourri, the petals are ready when they have become leathery.

**2** When you have enough rose petals to fill three cups to capacity, layer them in a large container with the salt, beginning with a layer of rose petals. Weigh down the mixture with a plate and weights. More rose petals and salt can be added over the summer. Leave for six weeks after the last flowers have been added.

**3** The mixture will gradually dry out. If any liquid forms, pour it off and save it; it will make a fragrant addition to your bath water.

**4** At the end of six weeks, the mixture should have become a dried-out cake of petals. Break this up in a large bowl and add the remaining ingredients. Mix well and seal in a plastic bag for four weeks so that the aromas can mingle. Store in an opaque container, and remove the lid when you wish to release the fragrance. Potpourri made by this method will retain its scent for many years.

## Dry method

The dry method of making potpourri is very simple and results in a more attractive mixture, as all the individual flowers and leaves are dried separately. However, the scents of the flowers are not as well preserved as in the moist method, so essential oils are usually added to the mixture. There is no single recipe for potpourri; simply try combinations that please you.

*rose petals and aromatic herbs, flowers, and*
*    leaves of your choosing*
*rosebuds*
*ground spices*
*citrus peels*
*orrisroot powder*
*essential oil(s)*

**1** Spread the petals and leaves on racks and leave in the hot sun or in a warm airy room until completely dry. Dry some complete rosebuds in the same way.
**2** Place the dried petals in a large mixing bowl and add the spices and citrus peels. Add about 1 ounce orrisroot powder to about every 10 ounces dried ingredients. The orrisroot will help preserve the scent of the other ingredients.
**3** Add your choice of essential oils one drop at a time, mixing well after each addition.
**4** Transfer the prepared potpourri into a large lidded container or sealed plastic bag and leave for six weeks to mature. Shake every other day. To refresh a potpourri that has lost its scent, shake it in a plastic bag with a few drops of essential oil.

## Fragrant flowers

*petals and flower heads*
*cotton ball (cotton wool)*
*essential oils*

To scent individual petals and whole flower heads, place them in a plastic bag with a cotton ball (cotton wool) onto which you have sprinkled several drops of essential oil. After two or three weeks, the flowers will have absorbed the scent of the oils.

## CUSHIONS AND SACHETS

Fragrant scatter cushions are intended to be a delight to the nose and the eye, but should also be soft and comfortable. When making a scented cushion, bear in mind that the potpourri should be crushed a little so that no sharp pieces poke through the fabric. There is no reason why you shouldn't slip a scented sachet into a favorite cushion, but it is satisfying to design and make your own covers.

If you decide to make your own cushion pad and choose a soft filling, such as duck or goose down, overstuff the cushion slightly, as it will flatten once it has been in use for a while. Slip the potpourri sachet between the pad and the back of the cushion. A less expensive alternative to down and feathers is to use a foam pad or two pieces of thick cotton wadding.

## Potpourri sachet

*enough muslin or thin cotton to make a sachet*
  *small enough to fit inside your chosen cover*
*cotton thread*
*pins*
*potpourri*

**1** Pin and tack two pieces of muslin together, leaving one edge open.
**2** Fill the sachet with potpourri and sew closed.
**3** If the sachet is to be visible, clip the corners and turn it inside out after step 1. Fill with potpourri, fold the raw edges in and press. Sew closed.

# Cushion cover with a center back zip

*enough fabric to cover the cushion pad*
*zip*
*cotton thread*
*pins*
*potpourri sachet*

**1** Cut the fabric into two pieces: the back piece should be 1½ in (4cm) longer than the front. Choose a zip that matches the fabric and that is 2 in (5cm) shorter than the width of the cushion.

**2** Fold the fabric for the back of the cushion cover in half across its width, and cut it along the fold to form two pieces. Place the pieces right sides facing and pin and tack together along one long edge to make a ¾ in (2cm) seam. Machine stitch 1 in (2.5cm) in from each edge of the seam.

**4** Pin the back and the front of the cushion cover together with right sides facing, then backstitch or machine stitch around the edges.

**3** Press the seams open then pin and tack the zip right side down over the wrong side of the open section. Turn the fabric over and, working from the right side, stitch the zip in position by hand using a backstitch, or machine stitch using a zip foot. Remove the tacking threads.

**5** Trim the seam corners and turn the cover the right side out, easing out the corners. Insert the cushion pad and the filled potpourri sachet through the opening, then close the zip.

# WREATHS

Making your very own fragrant wreath is a deeply satisfying experience. With a simple metal frame, some evergreen boughs, and a selection of spiced ornaments, you can create a wonderful addition to your home. The basic method given here is for a pine-scented Christmas wreath, but all kinds of evergreen foliage can be used.

## Pine wreath

*wire coat hanger or*
*    ready-made metal base*
*damp sphagnum moss*
*florist's wire*

*pine boughs*
*scented ornaments*
*    such as cinnamon*
*    bundles, dried citrus,*
*    bunches of herbs,*
*    and pinecones*
*ribbon*

**I** If using a coat hanger, carefully bend it into a circle, keeping the hook in shape. If using a ready-made base, make sure that it has a loop from which to hang it. If not, construct one from stiff wire.

**2** Bind bundles of damp moss around the frame with the florist's wire. Continue until the frame is evenly covered all the way round.

**3** Gradually add pine boughs to the moss-covered frame, taking care to conceal the bare stems.

**4** When satisfied with the base, attach the scented ornaments with more wire.

**5** Hang the wreath in its new home and make any final adjustments. Make a bow with the ribbon and attach it to the base of the wreath.

# BATHTIME

Using these bathtime products will make your skin fragrant and will fill the whole bathroom with wonderful, aromatic steam. The only rules about creating a fragrant bath oil are that essential oils should always be diluted in a pure, odorless carrier oil. The best of these is a treated castor oil called turkey red oil, which is available from pharmacists.

## Basic bath oil

*4 tbsp base oil, such as turkey red oil, almond,*
  *jojoba, or sunflower oil*
*approx. 20 drops essential oil(s) of your choice*
*a few drops food coloring (optional)*

**1** Pour the base oil into a sterilized bottle. Limit the essential oils to three or four, and add them a little at a time. Shake well.
**2** Leave for two weeks in a dark place for the scents to blend and mature. Decant into a pretty container and shake well before use. Add 1 tbsp to your bath when the water has reached the required temperature.

## Foaming bath oil

*4 fl oz (125ml) almond oil*
*4 tbsp mild, unscented liquid soap or baby*
  *shampoo*
*approx. 10 drops essential oil(s) of your choice*

**1** Pour the almond oil into a sterilized bottle.
**2** Add the liquid soap and shake well.
**3** Add the essential oil and shake again. Leave for two weeks for the scents to blend and mature. Add 2 tbsp to running hot water.

## Simple scented soap

*approx. 5 drops essential oil(s)*
*gauze or absorbent cotton fabric*
*unscented soap bar*

**I** Scatter a few drops of essential oil onto a piece of fabric.
**2** Wrap the fabric around the bar of soap and place in a plastic bag. Leave for two months and the soap will become delicately scented.

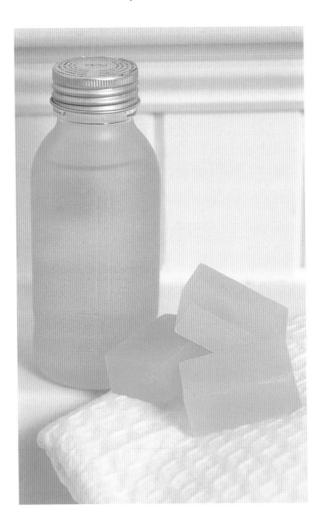

## Fragrant foot bath

*hot water*
*2 tbsp sea salt*
*approx. 20 drops essential oil(s)*

**I** Fill a bowl with enough hot water to cover your feet up to the ankles.
**2** Add the salt and swish it around until dissolved.
**3** When the water is a comfortable temperature, add the fragrant oils. Sit somewhere comfortable with your feet in the bowl and relax.

## Bath bag

*piece of muslin or thin cotton measuring about*
   *4 x 10 in (10 x 25cm)*
*cotton thread*
*fragrant herbal mixture of your choice*
*string or ribbon*

**I** Fold the material in half and machine sew along the long sides, leaving a seam ½ in (13mm) wide.
**2** Trim the corners and turn the bag inside out.
**3** Run a gathering stitch around the top of the bag about 1½ in (4cm) from the edge.
**4** Fill the bag with the herbal mixture.
**5** Pull up the gathering thread to close the pouch, and tie the ends. Tie the string around the closed neck of the bag, leaving a long loop so that the bath bag can be hung over the hot tap. Decorate with a pretty ribbon, if you wish.

# How-to Instructions
## *The Seasons*

PAGES
18-19

## Rosemary-flavored oil

*good-quality olive oil*
*clove of garlic*
*sprig of rosemary*

**I** Drop one whole, peeled clove of garlic into a bottle of oil and add a generous sprig of fresh rosemary. Store in a cool dark place. The oil will be scented and ready to use after a couple of months.

## Tarragon vinegar

*2–3 sprigs fresh tarragon*
*good-quality white-wine or cider vinegar*

Add the sprigs of clean, dry tarragon to a bottle of vinegar. Cork or seal the bottle and leave it for about three weeks, shaking occasionally. The vinegar will become delicately scented. If you intend to give the vinegar as a gift, strain it into a clean bottle and replace the herbs with fresh ones.

PAGES
28-29

## Lavender bunches

*approx. 50 pieces*     *scissors*
  *long-stemmed lavender,*    *decorated muslin*
  *dried*      *cotton thread*
*string*      *ribbon*

**I** Gather the lavender stems into a bunch and tie firmly with string.
**2** Cut a piece of muslin to about 2ft x 5½in (60 x 14cm) and fold in half crosswise. Sew along both the long sides, turn the right way out, and hem the bottom to prevent fraying.
**3** Carefully insert the bunch of lavender into the muslin pocket, and tie a ribbon around the stems.

## Citrus pouch

*essential citrus oil such*    *plate, about 12 in*
  *as grapefruit, lemon or*     *(30cm) in diameter*
  *orange blossom*     *tailor's chalk*
*scraps of white muslin*    *scissors*
*yellow and white*     *ribbon*
  *gingham fabric*

**I** Sprinkle several drops of essential oil onto the scraps of muslin.
**2** Place the piece of gingham right side down on a table. With the plate in the center of the fabric trace around it with the chalk. Cut out the circle of fabric.
**3** Place the scraps of muslin in the center of the circle. Gather the edges of the gingham together and fasten with a ribbon to create a pouch. Tie to the top of a coat hanger.

## Gingham nightdress case

scissors
blue and white gingham
cotton thread
daisy trim
muslin sachet

For the potpourri:

2 cups rose petals
2 cups lavender
1 cup myrtle
1 cup mock orange
    blossoms
1 cup violets
1 cup honeysuckle
1 tsp each ground
    cloves, cinnamon
    and allspice

**1** Cut three pieces of fabric approximately 1ft x 2ft (30 x 60cm). Hem one short edge of one piece of fabric. Sandwich this between the remaining pieces, right sides facing. Sew along the two long edges and short unhemmed edge.

**2** Fold back and hem the edges at the remaining short side, and turn the right way out. You will now have a sleeve with two sections: one to hold the nightdress, the other to contain a potpourri sachet. (See page 130 for instructions on making a sachet.)

**3** Fold back the edges at the open end of the sleeve and add the daisy trim.

PAGES
22-23

## Lemon cake

6oz (175g) butter
6oz (175g) caster sugar
6oz (175g) self-raising
    flour
3 large eggs, beaten
1 tsp baking powder
2 tbsp lemon curd
1 tbsp caster sugar
juice 1 lemon

For the decoration:

sprigs of mint
1/2 lemon, thinly sliced
1 egg white
5 tbsp caster sugar

**1** Pre-heat the oven to 200°F (100°C). Combine the butter with the caster sugar then sieve in the flour.

**2** Gradually beat in the remaining ingredients then pour the smooth mixture into a greased 8 in (20cm) cake tin.

**3** Cook for 30 to 40 minutes, or until golden brown. In the meantime, combine the caster sugar and lemon juice in a small bowl. When the cake is done,

remove it from the oven and drizzle the lemon mixture over the top. Leave to cool.

**4** To make the decoration, dip the mint leaves and lemon slices in the egg white, then sprinkle them with sugar. Shake off any excess sugar and leave to dry. Use to decorate the cooled cake.

> **IMPORTANT · If you plan to decant store-bought oils and vinegars into your own bottles, make sure that you sterilize the containers first. Wash and dry the bottles, then place them on their side on a rack in the oven. Leave them for about ten minutes at 100°F (40°C).**

PAGES
30-31

# Grapefruit body splash

*3½ tsp almond oil*
*4 drops grapefruit essential oil*
*½ tsp lecithin*
*¾ tsp witch hazel*
*4 tsp grapefruit juice*

**1** Pour the oils into a screw-topped glass jar and shake well.
**2** Add the lecithin, witch hazel and grapefruit juice and shake again. Refrigerate and use within one week. This amount makes enough for two showers.

**IMPORTANT** · Essential oils are very potent and should always be diluted in a carrier oil before use on the skin. Check for sensitivity by placing a drop of each chosen oil on the inside of your wrist and leaving it for 24 hours. If they cause an allergic reaction, do not use. Not all oils agree with everyone.

PAGE
33

# Herbal bath bag

*2 tbsp dried rosemary*
*1 tbsp dried lemon verbena leaves*
*4 oz (125g) cornmeal*

This mixture will fill eight to ten bath bags, and will remain fragrant for up four months. Rosemary is good for relieving tired limbs, while the lemon verbena is invigorating and aromatic. The cornmeal will soften the water and your skin. Make the bath bag following the method given on page 134, and discard after use.

PAGE
35

# Lavender-scented ink

*½ oz (15g) dried lavender flowers*
*6 tbsp water*
*1 small bottle ink*

**I** Crush the lavender flowers and place them in a saucepan with the water. Bring to the boil and simmer for about 30 minutes, or until you have 2 tbsp brown, opaque liquid.
**2** Strain, pressing down well. Mix the fragrant liquid with the ink.

SPRING

PAGES
48-49

## Ice bowl

*two bowls, one 2–3 in
(5–7.5cm) larger in
diameter than the other
mineral water*

*clean white pebbles
rose stems
masking tape*

**1** Fill the larger of the two bowls with 2 in (5cm) of water and freeze overnight.

**2** Place the small bowl inside the large bowl, and weigh it down with small pebbles to prevent movement. Place rose stems in the gap between the two bowls and tape them in place. Pour water into the gap so that it comes about halfway up the sides of the bowl, but below the tape. Freeze.

**3** Remove the tape: the roses should now be frozen in position. Fill the remaining gap with water and freeze overnight.

**4** To release the ice bowl, run it under the cold tap. Once released, put on a plate and keep in the freezer until needed.

## Crystallized rose petals

*fresh rose petals
egg white*

*caster sugar*

**1** Pick some white, pink and red rose petals making sure they are completely dry. (Place them on a tissue to absorb any excess moisture.)

**2** Dip each petal in the egg white, then completely cover it in sugar. Shake off any excess or the sugar will form ugly clumps on the petals.

**3** Spread the petals on a wire rack and leave them somewhere warm and airy to dry.

PAGE
39

## Floral swag

*evergreen foliage
florist's wire
wire cutters
roses
metal clips*

**1** Choose green leafy foliage such as soft ruscus to form the base of your swag and bind the branches securely with wire. Thread more greenery around the binding to obscure the wire.

**2** Once you are happy with the base, insert the roses into the swag. Attach the swag to the tablecloth with strong clips – not pins, which will tear the cloth. Make any last adjustments once the swag is fixed in position.

S U M M E R

PAGE
**51**

# Lemonade

*3 large lemons*
*4oz (125g) sugar, or to taste*
*1³/₄ pints (1 litre) boiling water*
*ice cubes*
*3 or 4 sprigs fresh mint*
*lemon slices*

**1** Chop the lemons into chunks and place in a heatproof container.
**2** Add the sugar and boiling water. Leave to cool.
**3** Strain over ice cubes into chilled glasses and decorate with the sprigs of mint and lemon slices.

PAGES
**52-53**

# Rosewater toner

*fresh rose petals*
*large glass jar*
*witch hazel*
*distilled water*

**1** Place fragrant rose petals in a large jar that you have first sterilized (see box page 137).
**2** Mix three parts witch hazel with one part distilled water and pour it over the petals so that the liquid covers and clears the petals by 2–3 in (5-7.5cm). Seal and leave in a warm, dark place for three weeks. Strain and pour into a clean bottle for use.

PAGE
**54**

# Organdy panels

*scissors*
*organdy*
*pins*
*cotton thread*
*tape measure*
*tailor's chalk*
*dried rose petals*

**3** Use the tape measure and chalk to divide the panel into equal sections and pin to prevent the fabric shifting.
**4** Stitch along the horizontal lines to create even sections in which to place a few scented rose petals.

**1** Cut two lengths of organdy fabric to the size required, then pin and tack them together.
**2** Stitch the two pieces together along the top and bottom edges. and sew down the center of the panel, leaving the sides open.

PAGES
56-57

## Rose-scented cushion

**For the cushion:**
*floral fabric*
*cotton thread*
*filling*
*zip*

**For the sachet:**
*muslin*
*cotton thread*

**For the potpourri:**
*2 cups rose petals*
*2 cups lavender*
*1 cup lemon verbena*
*1 tbsp rosemary*
*2 tsp cloves, crushed*
*1 tbsp orrisroot powder*
*3 drops rose essential oil*
*2 drops lavender essential oil*

This amount of potpourri will fill a sachet
approximately 8 x 10 in (20 x 25.5cm). Make up the
cushion cover and inner sachet by following the
instructions on pages 130-31.

PAGES
60-61

# Heart-shaped pomander

*florist's foam*  
*pencil*  
*knife*  
*wire*  

*ribbon*  
*dried, scented rosebuds*  
*(see page 129)*

**1** Draw a heart shape on the foam and cut it out with the knife. Don't worry if the edges are not completely regular, as this will be concealed by the rosebuds.

**2** Cut a piece of wire to just over twice the length of the heart. Bend it in half and thread the ribbon through the loop. Push the wire ends down through the top of the heart. Where they appear at the base of the heart, bend them back against the foam to secure.

**3** Push the stalks of the rosebuds into the foam, keeping them close together so that no foam shows through. When complete, tie a bow in the ribbon and hang where the pomander can be admired!

PAGE
42

# Scented book

*book made with plain,*  
  *handmade paper*  
*plastic bag*  

*potpourri sachet*  
*fresh summer flowers*  
*water-based craft glue*

**1** Place the book in a plastic bag with a potpourri sachet filled with your favorite flowers, and leave for two weeks.

**2** To dry some of your favorite summer flowers, use a flower press or place the flowers between sheets of blotting paper between the pages of a book. Stack heavy books on top and leave for two weeks, or until completely dry.

**3** Glue the flowers into the book and place tissue paper between the pages to create a fragrant souvenir of long summer days.

S U M M E R

PAGE
67

# Dried apple wreath

*10–15 red apples*
*juice of 6 lemons*
*1½ tbsp salt*
*aluminum foil*
*paper towels*
*wire*
*ribbon*

**I** Cut the apples into slices ⅛ in (3mm) thick. Pre-heat the oven to 250°F (120°C). Soak the apple slices for ten minutes in a bowl containing the lemon juice, salt, and enough water to cover the apples. In the meantime, cover wire racks with foil that you have perforated to allow for ventilation.

**2** Dry the apple slices with the paper towels and lay them on the prepared racks. Bake for five or six hours, turning occasionally so that both sides are evenly done. Remove when the slices are leathery, but not brown.

**3** Thread the slices onto wire, form into a ring and decorate with bows.

PAGES
64-65

# Aromatic scatter cushion

**For the potpourri:**

*2 cups rose petals*
*1 cup lavender*
*½ cup lemon verbena*
*½ cup thyme*
*½ cup rosemary*
*½ cup orange peel*
*1 tbsp cloves, crushed*
*2 tbsp cinnamon chips*
*3 drops bergamot*
  *essential oil*
*2 drops clove essential oil*
*1 drop cinnamon*
  *essential oil*

**For the cushion:**

*fabric*
*cotton thread*
*filling*
*zip*
*piping and tassels*
  *(optional)*

**For the sachet:**

*muslin*
*cotton thread*

This amount of potpourri will fill a sachet approximately 8 x 8 in (20 x 20cm). Make up the cushion cover and inner sachet by following the instructions on pages 130-31.

PAGES
70-71

# Apple pie

*8oz (225g) plain flour*
*pinch of salt*
*1 3/4 oz (50g) butter*
*1 3/4 oz (50g) lard chilled and cubed*
*1lb 9oz (700g) cooking apples*
*1 3/4 oz (50g) sugar*
*1 3/4 oz (50g) brown sugar*
*pinch grated nutmeg*
*1/4 tsp ground cinnamon*
*grated rind and juice of half a lemon*

**1** Mix the flour and salt in a bowl and lightly rub in the fat.

**2** Gradually add 3–4 tbsp of chilled water, mixing with a knife until a ball is formed. Wrap the dough in foil and leave it in a refrigerator for 30 minutes. Pre-heat the oven to 375°F (190°C).

**3** Peel and core the apples then slice them into a 2 pint pie dish. Sprinkle with the sugars, nutmeg, cinnamon, lemon juice, and rind.

**4** Roll out the pastry on a floured surface and cut a strip to fit the edge of the pie dish. Dampen the edge of the dish, then add the strip of pastry pressing it down firmly. Dampen the edges then lay the rest of the pastry over the pie to form a lid.

**5** Flute the edges and make a steam hole in the center. Use the pastry trimmings to make decorations. Bake for 35 to 40 minutes until the fruit is tender and the top is golden brown.

AUTUMN

PAGE
70

# Blackberry jam

*2lb (900g) blackberries*
*1lb 12oz (800g) sugar*

**Makes 6lb (2.7kg) jam and fills six 1lb (450g) jars.**

**I** Squash the blackberries in a large bowl, leaving a few fruits whole to give a nice texture to the jam. Transfer to a preserving pan and stew for 15 to 20 minutes.

**2** Stir, aiming to squeeze as much juice out of the fruit as possible. Add the sugar and stir until dissolved: if there are any granules of sugar left the jam will crystallize. Turn up the heat and boil rapidly for eight minutes, stirring occasionally to prevent sticking.

**3** To test whether the jam is ready, place a little on a chilled saucer and push it with your finger. If the skin wrinkles, the jam has set; if it doesn't wrinkle, boil for a further five minutes. Repeat as necessary. Meanwhile heat the sterilized jam jars in the oven. Pour the jam into the jars and leave to cool. Cover the tops with waxed paper discs and leave to set.

PAGE
72

# Toffee apples

*14oz (400g) soft brown sugar*
*4oz (100g) butter*
*2 tbsp water*
*12 red apples*
*12 wooden skewers*
*well-greased plate*
*red cellophane*
*red ribbon*

**I** Place the sugar, butter, and water in a saucepan and gently warm until the sugar has melted. Bring to the boil (275°F/140°C), stirring all the time. Test that the toffee is ready by dropping a teaspoonful into a saucer of cold water. If it forms a pliable ball, the toffee is ready.

**2** Spear the apples with wooden skewers or sticks. Dip the apples in the caramel, coating them evenly.

**3** Place the covered apples on the plate and leave to cool. Once cool and set wrap them in cellophane and tie with ribbons.

PAGES
**74-75**

# Spiced cider

*1³/₄ pints (1 litre) cider*
*1³/₄ pints (1 litre) cranberry juice*
*dash of brandy*
*1 lemon, sliced*
*1 orange, sliced*
*2 in (5cm) fresh ginger, peeled and sliced*
*2 tbsp sugar*
*6 cloves*
*¹/₂ tsp nutmeg, grated*

Place all the ingredients in a saucepan and bring to
a gentle simmer. Serve as soon as the mixture is hot.
Keep the cider warm for additional servings.

PAGE
**79**

# Pillow sachets

**For the potpourri:**

*1 cup lavender*  *1 cinnamon stick, crushed*
*1 cup lemon verbena*  *1 tbsp cloves*
*1 cup hops*  *5 drops lavender oil*
*1 cup rose petals*  *5 drops bergamot oil*

**For the sachets:**
*muslin*
*cotton thread*
*fabric roses*

This amount of potpourri will fill approximately four
sachets, about 6 x 4 in (15 x 10cm). Make up the
sachets by following the instructions on page 130,
but adding a flap as shown in the photograph. Fill
the sachets with the scented mixture, fold over the
flap and sew closed. Decorate with fabric roses.

PAGE
80

## Moth-deterrent sachets

**For the covers:**
*velvet*
*cotton thread*
*glass beads*

**For the sachets:**
*muslin*
*cotton thread*

**For the potpourri:**
*3 cups red cedar*
*shavings*
*1 cup lavender*
*1 cup rose petals*
*5 drops lavender*
*essential oil*

This amount of potpourri will fill approximately four sachets, about 4 x 4 in (10 x 10cm). Make up the sachets by following the instructions on page 130, and fill them with the scented mixture. Decorate the velvet cover with glass beads.

PAGE
81

## Autumn potpourri

*selection of woodland ingredients, for example, pine*
*cones, attractive pieces of dried wood, corn cobs*
*1 tbsp sandalwood powder*
*½ tsp powdered nutmeg*
*2 drops cypress essential oil*
*2 drops cedarwood essential oil*
*2 drops ylang-ylang essential oil*

Check the woodland ingredients for insects, then place in a plastic bag together with the combined scented ingredients. Shake well. Leave for two or three weeks before displaying in an attractive bowl.

PAGES
82-83

## Scented coat hanger

*1 cup dried lavender*
*1 cup dried rose petals*
*5 drops lavender*
*essential oil*

*fabric*
*wooden coat hanger*
*cotton thread*
*ribbon*

**I** Make up the potpourri in the normal method.
**2** Fold the right sides of the fabric together and place the coat hanger on top of it. Cut around the coat hanger, allowing 1 in (2.5cm) for the seams.
**3** Pin, then sew the seams together, leaving a large enough gap to insert the coat hanger. Turn the fabric the right way out.
**4** Slide the coat hanger into the shape then carefully pour in the potpourri.
**5** Sew up the gap and wind the ribbon around the metal hook. Fasten with a stitch.

PAGE
84

# Perfumed wash balls

*3 translucent and unscented soap bars*
*¼ cup hot water*
*approx. 6 drops orange or red food coloring*
*approx. 10 drops orange blossom essential oil*

**1** Grate the soap very finely into a heatproof bowl and add the water.
**2** Place the bowl in a saucepan and pour water into the pan. Place on a medium heat and stir occasionally until the soap is soft. Remove from the heat.
**3** Add a few drops of food coloring and essential oil to the soap and stir until well mixed.
**4** Leave the mixture for about ten minutes in a warm place until it is cool enough to handle. Divide it into three equal lumps and mold these into balls with your hands. Leave the wash balls in a warm dry place to cure for about four weeks before use.

PAGES
84-85

# Fragrant shoe sachets

**For the potpourri:**
*1 cup lavender*
*1 cup lemon verbena*
*½ cup rose petals*
*1 cinnamon stick,*
  *crushed*
*1 tbsp cloves, crushed*
*5 drops lavender*
  *essential oil*
*5 drops bergamot*
  *essential oil*

**For the sachets:**
*paper*
*velvet*
*cotton thread*
*ribbon*

**1** Use the soles of the shoes to create two paper templates for the sachets.
**2** Cut out two fabric shapes for each sachet, allowing 1 in (2.5cm) all round for the hem.
**3** Pin, then tack, the right sides together. Sew up the sachet, leaving a gap through which to insert the potpourri. Turn the sachet the right way out.
**4** Combine the herbs and the oils in the usual manner and spoon into the sachet. Sew up the gap, and add the ribbon. Repeat for the second sachet.

**AUTUMN**

**IMPORTANT • Pregnant women should consult a doctor before using any essential oils and should avoid all oils during the first three months of pregnancy. Pennyroyal, sage and wintergreen should not be used at any stage. After the initial three months, lavender and chamomile can be used in low dilutions.**
**Infants are very sensitive and should not be given potpourri-filled pillows.**

**4** Divide the dough into two parts and roll it out, one half at a time, on a lightly floured surface to a thickness of approximately ⅛ in (3mm).

**5** Use a cutter to make the star shapes then carefully make a hole in one of the points with a skewer (this is for the ribbon). Place the stars on lightly greased baking sheets.

**6** Bake at 375°F (190°C) for 12–15 minutes until golden brown. When cooked, leave on the tray for one minute then transfer to a wire rack to cool. You may need to push the skewer through the holes again to open them up after cooking. Carefully thread lengths of ribbon through the holes, then sprinkle each star with icing sugar

PAGES 106-107

## Gingerbread stars

*12oz (350g) plain white flour*
*1 tsp bicarbonate of soda*
*2 tsp ground ginger*
*4oz (125g) butter*
*6oz (175g) light brown sugar*
*1 egg, beaten*
*4 tbsp golden syrup*
*icing sugar (for decoration)*

**1** Sift the flour, bicarbonate of soda, and ground ginger into a large bowl then rub in the butter until the mixture is the consistency of fine crumbs. Stir in the brown sugar and make a well in the center.

**2** In another bowl, beat the egg and the syrup until evenly combined.

**3** Gradually pour the syrup mixture into the dry ingredients and mix to a fairly firm dough. Knead until smooth.

WINTER

PAGES
110-111

# Winter potpourri

| | |
|---|---|
| 1 large orange | 3 drops bergamot |
| 1 cup lavender stems | essential oil |
| 1/2 cup cedarwood chips | 2 drops lavender |
| 1/2 cup cloves, crushed | essential oil |
| 3 tbsp orrisroot powder | 2 drops neroli |
| 1 tsp cinnamon | essential oil |

**1** Cut the orange into thin slices and place on a baking tray that you have first covered with greaseproof paper.

**2** Place the slices in the oven at the lowest setting for about half an hour or until completely dried out. When cool, add to the potpourri mixture.

# Sleep pillow

**For the pillow:**
*velvet*
*cotton thread*
*tassels (optional)*

**For the sachet:**
*muslin*
*cotton thread*

**For the potpourri:**
*1 cup hops*
*1/2 cup linden*
*2 tbsp bergamot leaves*
*2 tbsp dried marjoram*
*2 tbsp dried lavender*
*2 tbsp dried chamomile*
*1–3 drops essential oil*
*(optional)*

This amount of potpourri will fill a sachet approximately 10 x 8 in (25.5 x 20cm). Make up the pillows and inner sachet by following the instructions on pages 130-31.

PAGE
120

# Christmas pudding

4oz (125g) currants
4oz (125g) chopped dates
4oz (125g) raisins
8oz (225g) sultanas
4oz (125g) chopped mixed peel
juice and grated rind of 1 orange
6oz (175g) butter
8oz (225g) brown sugar
2 medium eggs, beaten
8oz (225g) fresh breadcrumbs
2 tsp ground mixed spice
1 tsp grated nutmeg
1 tbsp flour
muslin
string

**1** Mix the dried fruit, peel and rind with the orange juice. Cover and leave to soak overnight.
**2** Cream the butter and sugar together until light and fluffy, then gradually beat in the eggs.
**3** Add the remaining ingredients and mix well.
**4** Place in the center of a floured pudding cloth and tie securely, but allowing room for expansion.
**5** Place the wrapped pudding in a large saucepan half filled with hot water and boil for four hours, topping up the water as necessary. Allow to stand for five minutes before serving.

PAGE
121

# Mulled wine

*2 bottles red wine*
*1³/₄ pints (1 litre) water*
*juice and rind of 1 orange*
*2 oranges, sliced*
*1 lemon, sliced*
*10 cloves*
*1 cinnamon stick*
*¹/₂ tsp grated nutmeg*
*2 tbsp brandy*

Place all the ingredients except the brandy in a large pan and simmer gently for ten minutes. (Do not allow to boil, as this will spoil the flavor.) Add the brandy, stir well and serve in warmed glasses.

## INDEX OF PROJECTS

## ACKNOWLEDGMENTS

Many thanks to Fast Flowers for supplying fresh flowers for the floral arrangements, and to Cameron Shaw for supplying dried flowers for the dried flower projects. Thanks to Laura Wilson and Michael Rimmer for lending us their home for the spring photographs, and thanks also to Angelic for allowing us to borrow candle holders. I should also like to thank my sister, Pip, for all her creative help with the projects. Her contribution has been invaluable.

## CREDITS

All photography by Shona Wood except for: © Garden Picture Library (G.P.L)/Ron Evans, p.16; G.P.L/John Millar, pp.24-5; G.P.L/Mayer/Le Scanff, pp.58–9; G.P.L/Brigitte Thomas, p.87; G.P.L/J. S. Sira, pp.88–9; G.P.L/Marie O'Hara, pp.104–5; G.P.L/Vaughan Fleming, p.113. © Emma Peios: endpapers, p.51 (bottom right), p.74 (top left), p.122 (bottom right).

The following images are copyright © Breslich & Foss Ltd: p.20 (bottom left), p.40 (bottom), pp.46–7, p.48 (top left), p.55, p.57, p.60, p.66, p.70 (top left), pp.76–7, p.129, p.135 (top left and right; bottom left), p.136 (top left), p.138 (center), p.139 (right), p.140 (top left), p.145 (right), p.150 (bottom), p.151 (top and bottom), p.152 (bottom).

*Illustrations by* Kate Simunek
*Book design by* Janet James
*Project manager*: Janet Ravenscroft